First published 2011
Set in Century Schoolbook 11 on 12.5
Published by Pasticcio Ltd. Registered in England No 5125728
01326 340153 www.pasticcio.co.uk

ISBN 978-0-9555511-8-5

Pasticcio

Bosvathick House

An introduction to its history

Stephen Tyrrell

Drawing Room,

Contents

Three pictures of Bosvathick showing the South and East fronts.

Introduction

Bosvathick is a small country house between Constantine and Falmouth.

This book describes the house, its grounds and the families of the house. It is a story not only of generations, but also of moneys made and lost. It is the story of a house which retains the appearance and historic features of life a century ago, but continues, as always, to be a family home, and the focus of family life. However, this is the story of the house and not of relations, their families and connections. Great chunks of adventure or interesting stories have necessarily been omitted because they did not relate directly to the house.

Since the 1760's, when the house, grounds and farms were re-assembled by the Moor or Muir family, Bosvathick has been lived in by their descendants and has never been sold. A period of 206 years passed under the name Horsford before the more recent change of family name to Tyrrell. The house has enjoyed some 250 years of occupation by one family.

This long occupation is also one reason why the house is so interesting. The decor reflects much of old fashions, and the clutter of papers, documents and trivia give life and interest to local architectural and social history and are important historic elements deserving of further study.

We hope that Bosvathick will long continue in the same family and that that family will continue to record changes in social and architectural history.

Small fields, little wooded valley, hills, streams and celtic field names record and link 1500 years of history at Bosvathick.

Chapter 1
Early History and Name

Bosvathick is to the North East of Constantine, towards Penryn and Falmouth. and was once one of many farming hamlets outside Churchtown. Cornwall was different in organisation to other parts of England in having no central village, but rather a scattering of farming hamlets connected by paths to the church and the couple of houses by the church. Thus, the modern village centre was always called the Churchtown, and the whole parish known by the name Constantine.

A rare survival is this early sign post showing the way to Constantine, quite properly referred to as *Churchtown.*

The paths to the church and the boundaries of the parish were marked by stones and crosses, nowadays considered rare survivals. There are three such gathered at Bosvathick. They probably date from the 7-9th centutries.

The Name

The name Bosvathick probably started as a 6th century farmstead, *Bos* being an early word for farmstead and Vathek the amended name of an early farmer, a Mr *Bothek* or *Boduc.*

One of three Crosses in the grounds of Bosvathick.

The spelling has varied through the centuries. The earliest written examples are *Boswodek* 1330 (Assize Roll), *Bosfothek* 1390, (Exeter MS); *Bosvathek* 1407 (deed in British Library), *Bosvothek* 1419 (Feet of Fines). The 'w- in the earliest spelling stands for 'v'. In Old Welsh a 10thC charter has the name Boduc in a 10thC charter copied into the 12th-century Book of Llandaf. Here the 'd' stands for 'th' (as in `then'). This corresponds to the Old Welsh Boduc (of unknown meaning), or may have some unknown meaning such as the later Cornish epithet *Bothek* (*Laurence Bothek `the humped*' 1327 in Paul parish).

Another name might be Budhyk (Budoc) a 'saint' who has named the village next door to Constantine. The 'uc' of the Welsh name does not however correspond closely to the -ek of the Cornish place-name, which was sometimes a diminutive, and some once suggested that the second half of the name might refer to some local feature such a a spring or small hill. Although there may always be discussion, Mr Oliver Padel's view that Bosvathick means the `*dwelling of (a man called) Bothek*' is now always accepted.

Early History

Bosvathick is set on a *plat* just down from a protective ridge and has shelter from the wind and a good water supply. It has a natural boundary, since it is on a small hill with water to all four sides. Bosvathick's story is one of a good site, some fields of reasonable soil, the interests of relatively few owners and a largely uneventful history.

On this site were two separate farms, one subsidiary to the other, and a couple of cottages or so.

Many fields still retain their Celtic names, suggesting a relatively unchanging settlement history. The boundaries have been the same for many centuries, although some fields have since became part of the surrounding woodland. More land seems to have been cultivated in the ealry 14thC than at any time since then. The acreage of Bosvathick has now been extended through the purchase of some neighbouring farms.

Bosvathick's story is therefore one of a good site, some fields of reasonable soil, the interests of relatively few owners and a largely uneventful history.

The first records of its history are from the 13th century, and show it was one of the larger farm holdings of the Parish. The owners had rights of armour and seem to have been of sufficient wealth and standing to pay fairly high taxes. Following the subdivision of manors it was held by semi-independent free tenants of the manor of Treworval.

In the late middle ages, the families or men who lived and worked a place took the name of their home as their surname. From the 13th century until the end of the 16th century the occupiers were always called Bosvathick. In 1407 and again in 1515 and 1525, deeds show that the *Bosvatheks* held considerable lands, some seven or eight farms, mills and other property. It was John Bosvothek with other members of his family who were there in 1522.

The Bosvathek family were lower gentry of some substance, but had fallen on hard times by the 1570s. Although the Bosvathek family ceased to own the place after the 1580s the family continued to live in the area.

Three gravestones in Glasney Church record the last of the Bosvatheks, who seem to have died out around 1840. Their name was by then spelt *Boswarthack,* a clue to the strong accent and pronunciation of a word with the emphasis on the second syllable.

In these four centuries, it is difficult to find evidence of much excitement at Bosvathick, unless you include the worries about arming against French or Spanish invasion in the sixteenth century or that day in 1613 when John Pendarves appeared before a church court for seducing Florence Tremayne.

"Here lyeth enterred the bodies of John Pendarves, gent. who departed this world the XVIth day of July 1616. And of Melior his wife, daughter of Richard Gearveis, esq., who departed this worlde the xvijth of March, 1607; children Samuel & Mary."

The Pendarvis Family and Subdivision

In 1587, *Boswathecke*, which had been mortgaged to them by John Bosvathick, was sold to the Pendarves family, who were on their way to becoming rich and powerful in Cornwall. One of the few remaining brasses in Constantine church is that from 1616 recording the death, Coat of arms and family of John Pendarves.
John Pendarves had done well with much property and mortgage speculation. He also owned at his death the site of Tywardreath Priory and part of the college buildings at Glasney, Penryn.

It was John Pendarves who was probably responsible for rebuilding the bigger farmhouse at Bosvathick in the 1590's. Victorian photographs and floor plans show that this was a "great rebuild" house with a chimney stack and massive fireplace at each end. It was a well built stone Tudor house, common in design and size to many in the area.

In 1620. the Pendarves family moved to Roscrow, on their way to becoming one of the mighty families of Cornwall. Bosvathick then became split among different tenants. The main farmhouse was leased to the Ley family who held it for three generations and then bought some parts of the property in 1660. Rents included 'a capon and work for a harvest day'.

The Ley family were of wide connection and considerable property, but seem to have used the main house at Bosvathick as their family base. However, from the end of the 17thC onwards, the two main farmhouses and accompanying houses and holdings, had a number of occupiers, divisions, sales, transfers and mortgages. This was partly in order to achieve division on marriage settlements, but also reflected the decline of the central interest and family.

The holdings were sub divided and decayed until taken over by Thomas Moor around 1760-1767.

"Bosvathick, the residence of Thomas Moor"
This water colour was found in a large portfolio of drawings all dating from around 1782, and thought to have been by one of the Moor family. The new house can be seen with its walled and fenced front garden, balls and pillars and the main farmhouse just in the background.

"The south east view of Bosvathick, with Mayne rock hill on the left and Paleston Carne to the right".
This drawing was probably done around 1800. The house still has the front door in the centre, one farm house can be seen behind the house and another to the left. The house still has the straight chimneys of first design.

The earliest photograph taken shortly after 1880 shows the blocked central door, and the chimney end of the old farmhouse wing and servant area just to the left. The farm yard, town place and front garden to the house have been removed.

Chapter 2
The Development of House and Grounds

The gothic arch by Nash that crossed the coast road, seen from the west.

The farming hamlet which Thomas Moor had bought in the 1760s was to be the site of his new country house, or villa. The existing site had two farmhouses, separated by a yard with a well. Both farmhouses were tucked into the hill, and there were also ranges of farm buildings and probably a cottage or two. Some idea of the farm and hamlet layout can be gained from the earliest plans of 1820, which are on a subsequent page.

The Gerogian House of 1760

Thomas More built a five bay villa in front of the eastern of the two farm houses. This design included a large central door, reached up a couple of steps, and over the door a fanlight. A short entrance corridor had a saloon to each side, each with two good windows. To the rear of these rooms were, to the north a neat Georgian stair, and to the right a rear extension with its own fireplace, which may once have been a kitchen or serving area. There is a small blocked window to the left of the fireplace and a further blocked opening in the north west wall. The central door was wider than the window bays, but generally the house was a neat and competent piece of design with coursed granite to the front over a high base plinth and with wide eaves above. The windows had early multipane sashes with simple mouldings. Examples of the window sashes have survived to be reused in the estate offices. Chimneys were set at each end and to the rear of the building to heat all the rooms.

The old farmhouse was a fairly standard late Elizabethan house, of c1590 with rabbit ear chimneys to each end, one end having the large chimney normal for a yeoman's farm kitchen. Quite unusually, plans of this old house exist, because it was surveyed before it was demolished in 1880. A service yard surrounded by a wall lay between the new Georgian villa and the farmhouse.

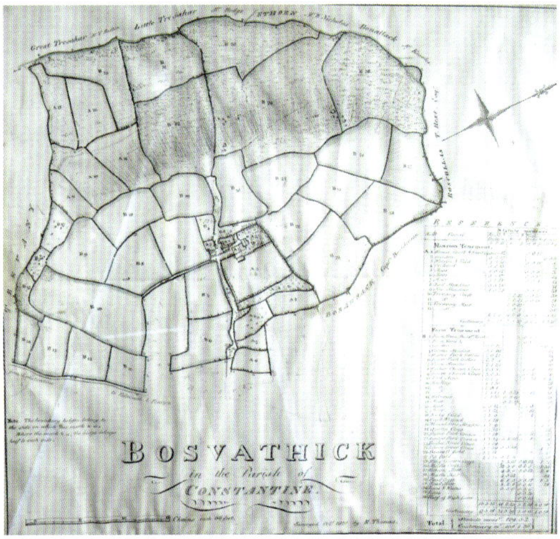

The earliest plan of the farm and buildings which we have was drawn from a survey by Richard Thomas of Falmouth in 1820, and includes details and sizes of each field. A detail of the house and farm layout is shown to the right.

Another version of the Bosvathick Farm map, circa 1820

This plan, drawn in 1870, shows proposals for the drive.
The western farmhouse is still in place.

Towards the south was built a small 30metre deep front garden. This had a low wall with shaped granite copings and above a fine iron rail which met at two pillars each side of an entrance gate. We have one picture of the house at this time, a picture thought to have been painted around 1782.

The new entrance front, probably taken around 1880, and showing the rebuilt chimneys, blocked south door, new porch and dining room, single story wing and the HaHa before the house.

At this time, the house and the old farmhouse to the rear retained some land to support the household, and the owners took part in some farming activity. As the 18thC ended, the house was altered to make it both larger and to provide better servant access.

The old farmhouse was joined to the Georgian block by a new dining room wing of one story with lumber rooms and stores in the attic. To one side was included a service corridor which allowed the farmhouse to be used as the kitchen with service along the corridor. The yard layout was changed and there were other extensions in the yard between the houses.

In the decades running up to 1870 a number of other alterations were made. Tanks were added for the supply of water, and drainage systems, some of which are still in use, installed around the house.

A picture of similar date which shows the addition of the conservatory and in the background the Elizabethan farmhouse and its chimney.

In 1848, TM Horsford had a three day sale of the contents of the house, and it is therefore assumed that shortly after some improvements and alterations were made. In 1860 he made a continental tour and it is following this that it is thought the first scheme of redecoration to the interior was carried out.

From then on, alterations proceeded apace. First, new smart chimneys were built and the east, or present entrance front, probably given a new facade. Then a large conservatory was added to the south west corner, and the small garden to the south enlarged by the removal of the balls and pillars. By 1890, the old front door had been removed, the opening narrowed and a window inserted. This allowed the new porch to be built with a changed entrance drive arriving on the east side of the house. Around this time the west saloon to the south was joined to the former hall corridor to make a larger room. Some of the plasterwork in the house may date from 1870 – 1880 rather than the final rebuild of 1896.

The south side of the porch thought to have been added in the 1880s.

In 1880 the second farmhouse and farmstead at Bosvathick was demolished to allow greater privacy and larger gardens. Bosvathick Farm was then re-built on its present site in 1880 as a new “model farm”. In these years also, the drive was improved and from 1884 given a smart little Lodge on the road.

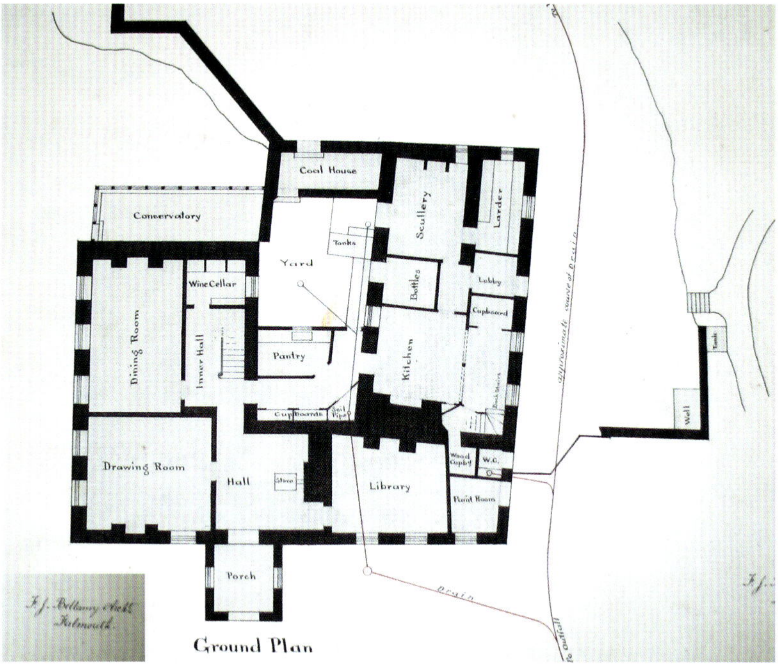

A plan by F J Bellamy in 1896 of the old house at Bosvathick, with the farmhouse to the rear.

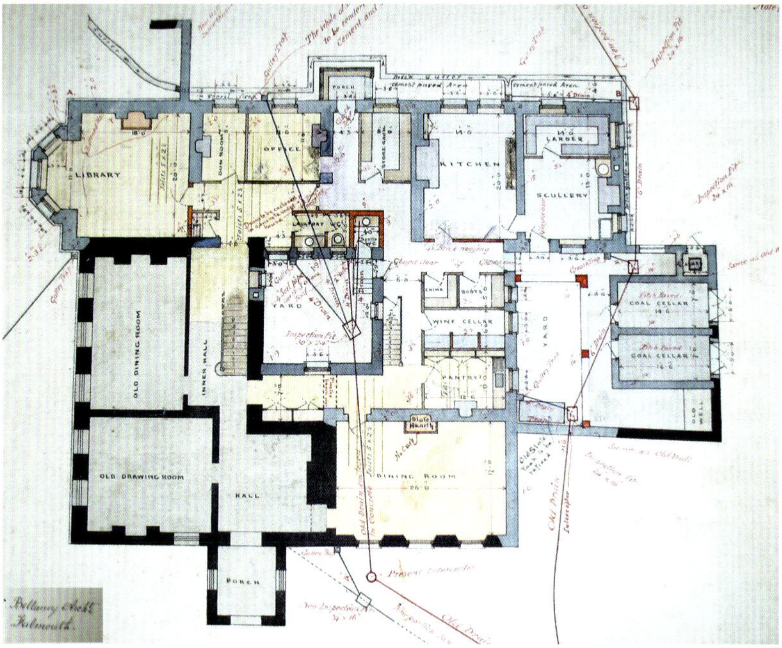

The proposals for the 1896 alterations at Bosvathick, by F J Bellamy, with working notes.

It was probably also at this time that a number of efforts were mde to improve the water supply to the house. There had been two wells at Bosvathick, one of which is still in use today. However, placed on the top of the hill, there was insufficient water for so large a house. Storage tanks were built around the garden, but efforts were also made to pump water from the streams below the house. There are still the remains of two different pumping stations and of a hydraulic ram which was intended to solve the problem.

The Rebuild and Extension of 1896

TMA Horsford had many ideas for improvement and in the 1880's commissioned designs for the renovation of the main house from Silvanus Trevail, who was perhaps the most famous architect of his day in Cornwall, and whose work is still much admired. He produced some beautiful coloured drawings set on oiled paper. They show a layout not that dissimilar to the eventual design. However, the Trevail scheme appears better thought through in use and practicality of the staff areas. Depite the advantages of the scheme, the design was not used and the rebuilding was delayed.

In 1896 the architect F. J. Bellamy was asked to prepare a full set of plans and building specifications. Franklin Joseph Bellamy, who was born about 1870 and lived to 1940 was, in 1890 still a reasonably young man but already the surveyor for Falmouth and, working with WH Tresidder, was the architect for the 1895 Passmore

An 1880s view of the house showing the old front door replaced by a window, the new porch, great lawn and conservatory to the north west.

Library in Falmouth. It was presumably through this work at Falmouth that he was became known to TMA Horsford. Little is known of his work or of his career after this date, since he moved away to the home counties.

F.J.Bellamy's detailed plans for the alteration and extension of the house were accepted, and he drew up detailed specifications. The building conditions and terms are similar to those in use today and remind us that little changes through the years. Some two inches thick and in beautiful copperplate, they cover terms of contract and all the details for each piece of work and each trade.

The drawings show that the Elizabethan house was demolished and replaced by a new kitchen wing. The old courtyard was retained, as was the service corridor down the west side of that yard. In addition to a new first floor above the old dining room and to rooms of greater height which meant that steps were necessary to corridors of the first floor, the principle extension provided a large bayed library on the ground floor to the west, with an owners bedroom and adjoining dressing rooms above it. Fortunately, all the contracts, bills and suppliers brochures for this work have been retained in the archive.

"The Moorish Arch"
The design for a screen to allow the drawing room to be extended to include the southwest saloon was prepared by Maple and Co, of London in 1899. The cost, with extra carvings, was just under £13.00. The work was carried out and the screen can still be seen in position today.

These two pictures show different ends of the main south drawing room. The photograph to the left shows the west end in September 1901. It is extraordinary to consider that in 2011, much remains the same, save that the harp has moved from the right to the left of the fireplace.
The picture to the right shows the 'Moorish Arch' ordered in 1899 which allowed the hall and the rooms to each side on the south front to become one long drawing room. The eastern end, seen here through the arch, was once designed as a Japanese room, and later became a billliard room.

The redesign also formalised the division between family and staff wings. The house remained a building that was in essence only one room thick, built around a corridor that on each floor ran round the edge of the internal yard. The work necessarily required interior redecoration, and there is some splendid plasterwork. There is also evidence of sensible economy in the panelling to the front hall, which almost no one notices is in fact of thick parchment wall-paper rather than timber.

The work was so extensive that much of the house and the interior decoration now appears Victorian, although the shell of the Georgian house remained untouched. Still in store however, and for us to admire, are pieces of the joinery and mouldings that had formed part of the 1760 Georgian design.

Few alterations were carried out until the 1980s. However, a boiler room for limited coal fired heating was installed in a new extension in the central yard in 1907. In 1923 two coal sheds were converted for use as a generator room and battery store to provide electricity to the limited wiring that was then being run through the house.

Later alterations have included inserting an arch in the kitchen yard wall which allows access to the kitchen door, the fitting of modern kitchens and the conversion of small servant bedrooms to provide bathrooms.

The Georgian stair was replaced by a grander and larger Victorian case with heavy moulded newels

Few alterations were carried out in the 20thC. This photograph shows the window that replaced the old front door on the south front. The work necessary to narrow the width can still just be seen. This photograph of April 1958, commemorates the addition of the circular steps agains the window, which can therefore be used as a garden door. The steps were taken from a farm at Trewoon, Budock.

A view of the south front showing the new library wing with Tommy and Nellie Horsford sitting proudly on their crocquet lawn, c1904.

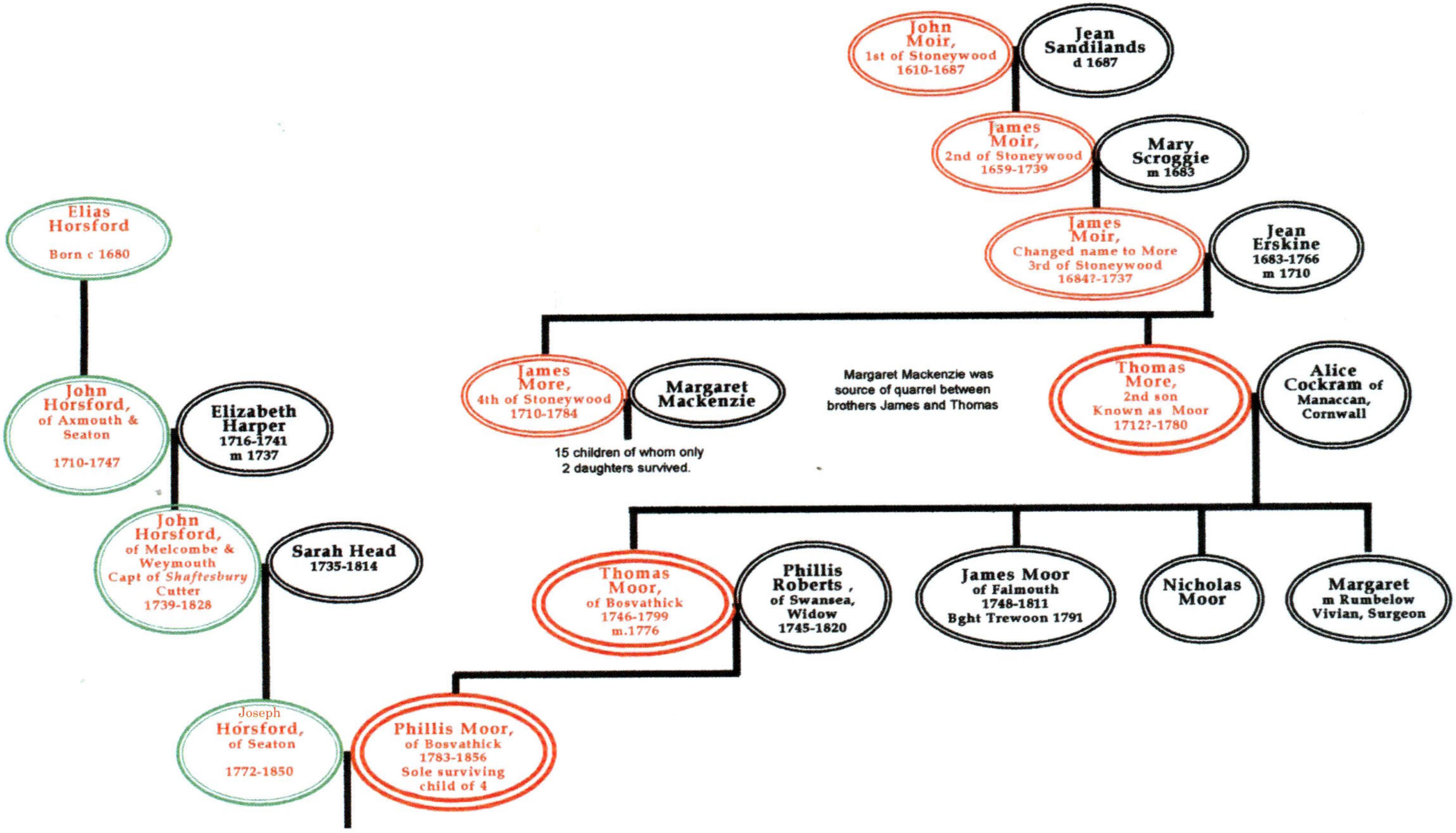

The family tree of the Muirs, or Moors until the time of their marriage into the Horsford family

Chapter 3
The Moor Family

Thomas Moor, who was described as a merchant, was the second son of an important Scottish family called Muir. His early life could be re-writen as a historical romance. Thomas is said to have left home, running away to Holland because of a bitter dispute with his older brother about a woman - (Margaret McKenzie McKenzie of Ardross).

This portrait, of which there is an identical copy, is possibly Captain Thomas Moor: 1746-1799.

Thomas's family had been 'proscribed' following both the 1715 and 1745 Scottish rebellions. This connection carried some risk for Thomas and was the reason for the changes in his family name. He seems to have started work as a sailor or adventurer on board ships, and became master of a ship from Aberdeen which was lost in the Mediterranean. He was in London in 1744 and thereafter went out as master of a privateer commanded by Capt. Sutherland after which he was supposed to have been lost on the coast of France. However, he survived and become a merchant with valuable interests of his own, based in Falmouth because of its good sea connections and because it was far from London and Scotland where his family name was not acceptable. It was in Falmouth that he met a wealthy widow, Alice Cockram of Manaccan and then decided to establish himself as a country gentleman.

Thought to be James Moor, a barrister of Falmouth and Thomas's brother: 1748-1811.

Trustees acting for Thomas, (who had changed the spelling of his name) re-assembled the four or five different tenancies and farms at Bosvathick in the 1760's. Deeds are signed 17 November 1761 and 24 June 1762, with negotiations for assembling the different pieces of tenure continuing for some years. There were transactions in 1772 and the trust may have been brought to an end in 1782. The family tradition is that building of the house commenced in 1760, and it seems that that portion of the lands on which it was built was the first acquired. Almost immediately was then built a fine Georgian House in the modern style some twenty yards to the south of the larger of the two farmhouses. A watercolour of that time gives a picture of this house and the old approach from the south west. Although always reticent about his past, Thomas lived to enjoy his new house at Bosvathick for some 20 years.

This was the home of his four children, Thomas a sea captain who inherited the estate, James who became a lawyer based in Falmouth, Nicholas a third son and a daughter, Margaret.

It is thought that the four matching portraits in Bosvathick dining room, with clothes of around 1760, are probably portraits of these four children. The second Thomas Moor, Captain Thomas, married a widow from Swansea. He died in 1799 leaving the only surviving child of four children as his heir. This heiress was, in 1801, married to Joseph Horsford at Constantine Church.

Their eldest son was named Thomas Moor Horsford and the use of the name Moor continued in the family name until the death of Corraleen Mary Moor Horsford in 2005.

Thought to be Nicholas Moor, the brother of Thomas and James.

Thought to be Margaret Moor, as a young girl. She was sister to Thomas and James and married Dr Vivian, a Surgeon of Falmouth

Long thought to be a portrait of Thomas Moor, of Bosvathick, 1746-1799, but possibly misidentified.

Phillis Moor, of Bosvathick, 1745-1820
Wife of Capt Thomas Moor of Bosvathick.

These two portraits are thought to be of the last Moors to live in Bosvathick. It was their daughter who inherited and married Joseph Horsford.

Chapter 4
The Lost Lands of Scotland

When Thomas Moor purchased the estates of Bosvathick in the 1760s he was known as a merchant and seafarer who had accumulated considerable wealth. He was reticent about his ancestry, and this was probably because he came from a family who had supported Jacobite rebellions agains the crown in both the 1715 and 1745 rebellions.

In fact his father and grandfather had fought in both these rebellions and both had been listed in a bill of attainder -or treason- by the British Government. This was the reason for the changing of the spelling of the family surname from Moir to More and then, in Falmouth, to Moor. It may also have been why he remained in Falmouth, far from a seat of power, avoiding contact with his relatives. Another reason may have been that he had quarrelled with his elder brother over a woman, to whom the older brother was eventually married.

However that brother was the 4th Lord or Baron of Stoneywood, who possessed a mansion at Stoneywood, outside Aberdeen and what had been described as many estates and 'broad acres' of Scotland. The family had certainly owned several thousand acres of useful land and farms earlier in the 18thC.

The Moirs had long been of importance in Scottish politics and activities. The Aberdeen Baillie books of the 15thC century record the names of Moirs who appear to have been substantial burgesses. A later John Moir went to Poland where he amassed a fortune. On his return he bought estates and in 1670 the estate of Stoneywood. The next couple of generations produced MPs, office holders and men of influence and John 2nd of Stoneywood assisted in the agreement of the Act of Union. However, fortune seems to have abandoned the family through their exile and absent management and through their support for Jacobite causes.

The brains seem to have drifted out of the family with the third James of Stoneywood who was outlawed after the 1715 rebellion in which he commanded a corp of Macdonads before fleeing abroad. He returned after an act of indemnity. His adventures are said to have included the rescue of a friend from the Tower of London through his servant carrying the man out in a barrel. It was because of the attainder that James Moir, 3rd of Stoneywood changed the spelling of his surname to *More* and caused all his children to do likewise.

Despite the opposition of his wife, who poured boiling water over his leg to try and prevent him leaving, the next James of Stoneywood, the 4th, raised a regiment for Bonnie Prince Charlie and joined him in the attack on England and at the battle of Culloden. He then had to flee the country after many romantic adventures, enduring disguises and hairbreadth escapes suitable for a novel. His early 'secret' correspondence from the continent is of financial difficulties only relieved when the French King gave him a grant of 1500 louis. Outlawed from Britain, he went to Gothenburg where he maintained himself as a merchant for sixteen years and received a patent of nobility from the King of Sweden. Returning to Scotland in 1762, he recovered Stoneywood. His last twenty years were spent in attempting to rebuild his fortunes, including a merchant agreement for a papermill near his main mansion, and attempts to sell the estate to his relatives. None of his 7 sons survived his death in 1784.

The male heir was therefore his eldest nephew, the son of his brother Thomas Moor. However, that Thomas Moor had died in 1780. In his search for financial rescue James of Stoneywood visited Bosvathick in 1782. His nephew Thomas visited Scotland in his turn. In a letter to his wife Thomas suggested he could really enjoy life up there. The correspondence also includes realistic letters from solicitors pointing out that his relatives were in poor health and unlikely to survive, so that Thomas could expect to inherit. James tried to persuade Thomas and his brother to buy Stonywood and the other estates- but not only was there a chance Thomas would inherit anyway, but he explained that he could not afford this.

When James died Thomas, now the legal heir, fought his claim to his Scottish inheritance and a swathe of Aberdeenshire. Much of the Scottish land had already been sold or so mortgaged as to be difficult of recovery. The main house at Stoneyhouse was put on sale in 1784, just before the death of James the 4th of Stoneywood. At the same time he executed a deed in favour of his daughter Jean who married George Skene of Rubislaw and after the death of James 4, took what was not sold with her to Rubislaw.

Despite their refusal to purchase the lands and house at Abedeen from their destitute uncle, Thomas and James had no doubt hoped to inherit as the legal male heirs of the Stoneyhouse estates. However, this was not to be.

Perhaps because the estates were too greatly encumbered and because of trusts set up for the surviving daughters it seems there was little worth fighting for. It may also be that because the lands were held of the government, they did not encourage the Moor case. The family tradition is that they lost their inheritance because of the change in the spelling of their surname. It seems possible therefore that the government took their share. The surviving correspondence with solicitors to establish whther he had a proper claim, suggested that in any case he had not a hope.

The family at Bosvathick have carefully kept all the correspondence for a further 220 years in the hope that there will be a change in heart on the rulings of the 1790s. One day, we shall surely recover those broad acres of Aberdeen and the oil rich regions of Scotland which are rightfully and delightfully ours.

Examples of correspondence from the 1780s and 1790 with family and solicitors about the Scottish inheritance.

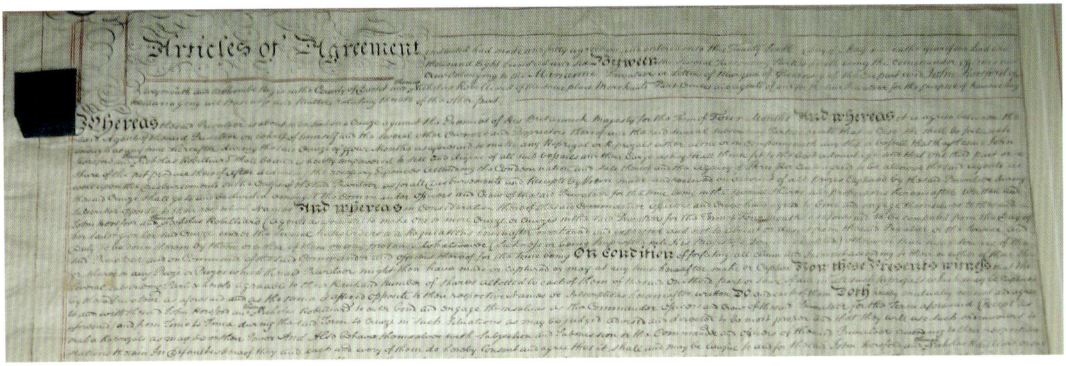

Articles of Agreement

Surviving short term contracts for the rent of a privateer are rare.This 1806 contract is between John Horsford and Thomas Nicholas Robillard for the use of the Marianne Privateer of Guernsey as a Letter of Marque.

A drawing of the famous action of 1807. A Falmouth packet boat, the *Windsor Castle* under the young William Rogers fought off the French privateer, *La Genie* which had more guns and 86 men to Rogers' 24. Rogers then boarded and won the French ship with just 12 men.

Chapter 5
Privateers, Ships and Fortune

A splendid silver tankard inscribed *"The gift of Warren Lyle Esq. to Captain John Horsford for his spirited conduct in taking the La Guine French Ship from Martinico bound to Bordeaux 1778."*
The engraving shows *La Guine* on the left and the *Shaftesbury* on the right. The large tankard can hold four imperial pints and was made in London by Charles Wright in 1778.
Warren Lyle was the famous surveyor of sloops on the south coast from 1740-1779

Ships and trade have been the life blood of Britain for centuries. Trade and dealing in ships and their contents were the business of many ports along the south coast. Fortunes could be made or lost in a single voyage by these small ships.

Both the first Thomas Moor and the Horsford Family ventured in ships. Often such ventures were just that, with financiers being called 'Adventurers'. They might be land based investors or merchants, but often started by voyaging as supernumeraries or working their way up to become Captain of a merchant ship. Both sides of the family invested in ships, the charter of ships and in the finance of *Privateers.*

The wars of the 17thC and 18thC produced trade confusion around the seas of Europe. Elizabeth 1 of England played havoc with the trade of her enemies. A tradition of licensed piracy developed over the next 200 years. It was not England alone who financed and benefited from privateers. The French, for instance made it a major industry, with the King of France taking a mammoth 25% share of any prize. St Malo and the great houses around it were all financed by this trade.

The small private men of war of the south coast had developed from that first English Navy where boats were hired in as needed. This need continued when the Navy failed to provide adequate protection and when trade required boats that could defend themselves not only against pirates, but against the traders of other nations. The coast of Cornwall had been long attacked by the ships of the French, Spanish and of coure the 'moors', who raided not only for goods but for slaves. In addition to the need for vessels that could defend themselves, it became commonplace for the government to issue 'Letters of Reprisal' or 'Letters of Marque' which authorised the holder to seize vessels at sea when outside the boundary or jurisdiction of the crown. In time the two terms became interchangeable and a *letter of marque* was issued to the venturer and captain of a 'privateer'. This was justified by the theory that people had suffered loss at the hands of a foreign power, but in practice reflected the interminable wars in which Europe and its trade colonies were engaged, or the existence of actual war with a neighbour.

Such Letters of Marque brought in sums to the government in a duty on the value of the goods and an additional 10% levied by the court doing the valuation. The remainder of the value of goods or ships sold was divided according to lengthy, complex agreements setting out the percentages which each faction might have, from financier, to captain and to junior crew. The financier or owner usually got a very substantial two thirds of the sum and this was after the expenses of the cruise had beeen deducted. He did however have to stand the losses of an unsuccessful voyage.

The privateer and the letter of Marque were a way of making a fortune, so long of course as you were succesful. Voyages were usually of short duration, limited by the expectation of the men and the available food, so that few contracts and agreements seem to survive.

Two such agreements do however survive at Bosvathick. One is a contract from 1806 between John Horsford and Thomas Nicholas Robillard for the use of the Marianne Privateer of Guernsey as a Letter of Marque. The other is a document recording the granting of a Letter of Marque by George III in February 1793 for the Brilliant cutter, financed by the Horsford family.

This authorised action aginst the enemy France by Samuel Smetham *'fitly qualified, who hath equipped, furnished and victualled a ship called the "Brilliant" cutter of the burthen of 46 tons, having a square stern, plain Head and 1 mast mounted with 8 carriage guns, carrying shot of 6 pounds weight and 4 swivel guns and navigated with 26 men of whom one third are landsmen and belonging to the port of Weymouth, whereof he, the said Samuel Smetham is Commander and Messrs Horsford and Gouvain of Weymouth, merchants are the Principal... and whereas we... issue forth a grant letter of Marque and Reprisals to and do licence and authorise the said Samuel Smetham to set forth in a warlike manner the said ship called the "Brilliant" cutter under his own command and therewith by force of arms to apprehend, seize and take the Ships, Vessels and Goods belonging to France or to any persons being subjects of France or inhabiting within any of the Territories of France."*

Other shipping activites which produced profit were of course smuggling and acting against smugglers fo the revenue. The first two members of the Moor fam-

The most famous of packet captains was John Bull, who, in his ship, the Marlborough, fought off attackers. He went on to make a fortune from packets and privateering and built Marlborough House in Falmouth. Phoebe, the daughter of his second marriage, married T.M.A.Horsford of Bosvathick.

ily who operated from Falmouth made large sums in trade and shipping although it is not always clear how. The Horsfords made trade, but also took contracts from the government against smugglers and financed a large number of privateers.

Part of an engraving showing how small was Falmouth town in 1806

John Horsford, 'Master Mariner and once Captain of the *Shaftsbury* cutter' distinguished himself in 1778 by the capture of the French ship *La Guinne* a vessel of superior size and armament. In this action Captain Horsford was in a 14 gun single masted cutter and took a larger three masted 18 or 24 gun ship.

Falmouth was also the base for much of the Packet service, the government postal service that linked the colonies and administration in both war and peace. Packet ships were intended to be fast and to fight off opposition. Not meant to carry trade, the captains had the habit of taking small amount of valuables from which they could do well. Most packet captains did indeed do well. Books on the packet trade abound, but the most famous and illustrious captain was John Bull, who in his ship the 'Marlborough' fought a great action to ensure the safety of his ship. He went on to manage and run a number of ships and packets. It was to John Bull's daughter that Thomas Moor Horsford was married, ensuring almost a century of close family activity by different family branches in the profits of trade, the sea and licensed piracy.

Although members of the wider family continued to ply the waves. that connection with the sea seems to have ended in the 1840s.

The SS Doretta under full sail and flying the flag of Captain Charles Atherton Folliott Powell, a Horsford family relation and business connection showing the importance of ships and trade to the family well into the 19thC.

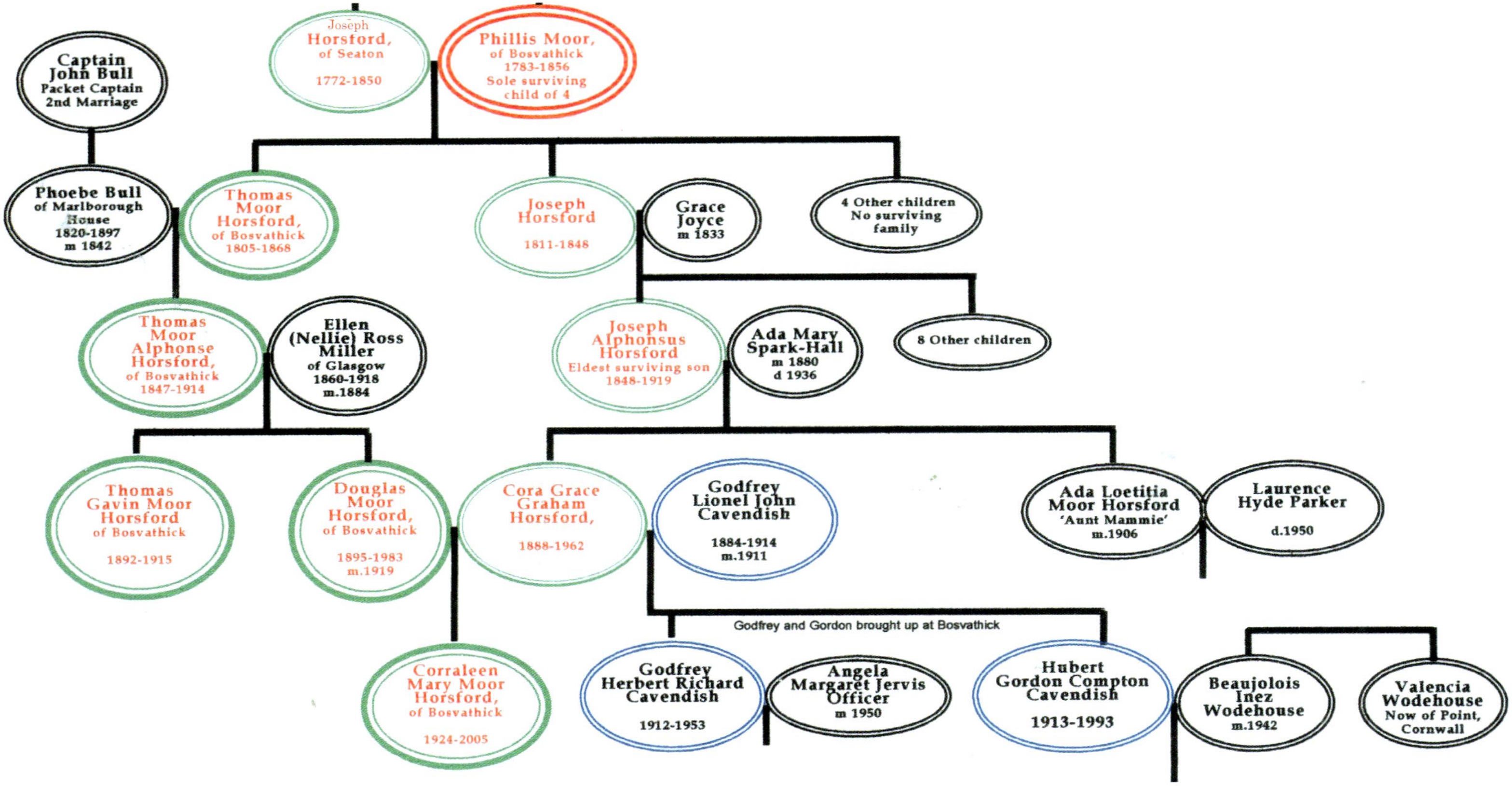

The Horsford Family from 1800 to 2005

Chapter 6
The Horsford Family

Early records of the Horsford family show that they came from the Axminster, Seaton, Weymouth and Melcombe area of the south coast and were merchants and traders. John Horsford the second (1739-1828) was a successful privateer captain and merchant, and it is thought it was he who laid the basis for the Horsford wealth. He purchased land in Dorset from Sir John Trevelyan, Bt, in 1787.

Joseph Horsford
1772-1850

Joseph Horsford (1772-1850)

His son, Joseph continued to finance merchants and privateers, and added to that wealth. His portrait suggests a canny businessman. He married the only surviving child of Captain Thomas Moor of Bosvathick and his wife Phillis. The daughter and heiress was a girl 11 years younger than Joseph and also called Phillis. They had presumably met because her father, based in Falmouth, was another ship owner.

Joseph, based in Weymouth had a succesful role in the public life of Dorset. He was a J.P., Lord of the Manors of Berne and Morcombe-Lake, and held many consular titles, including among others, those of Royal Hanover, France, Prussia, the Netherlands and Portugal. These appointments were an important way to profit from the ships and trading of other nations.

Mrs Phillis Horsford
(Nee Moor)
Wife of Joseph Horsford
1783-1856

Joseph was a strong Tory politician who was several times Mayor of Weymouth. He bought land around Morecombe, Weymouth and Seaton which he and his heirs were able to build on. Horsford Street in the borough was named after Joseph. The last sales of Horsford land in Dorset took place in the 1960s.

Joseph was also a Captain of Volunteers during the Revolutionary and Napoleonic Wars. He was wealthy enough to make a point of refusing the pension offered him on his relinquishing the 'Agency of the Portland Lights'.

Joseph and Phillis had four sons and two daughters. The eldest, John was chaplain and secretary to the Foreign Secretary, the Earl of Aberdeen, and looked set fair for a career in politics.

His portraits show an unusually cheerful and pleasant man. Sadly he did not survive and his young son also died so that the second son Thomas Moor Horsford inherited. For much of this time it is thought that Bosvathick was a second home and the farms rented out. It is not clear why this was the home chosen by Thomas Moor Horsford as his principal residence.

Important to todays family at Bosvathick was the next son of Joseph and Phyllis, also called Joseph (1811-1848). In 1919, their grand daughter Cora Horsford married her cousin Douglas Horsford of Bosvathick, himself the grandson of Thomas Moor Horsford, thus bringing together in direct descent the two arms of the family descended from the marriage of Joseph Horsford and Phillis Moor.

The youngest son of Joseph and Phillis Horsford is represented by two portraits in the Dining Room. One portrait of considerable size shows Arthur Wellington Horsford (1814-1847) in the Mayoral robes of Weymouth. He looks as though he thought a lot of himself. Successful in business and local politics, he died in Georgetown, British Guiana, where he he was on government service.

Thomas Moor Horsford as a young man
1805-1868

Phoebe Bull, 1820-1897
wife of Thomas Moor Horsford, Daughter of Packet Captain John Bull.
Portrait at time of marriage in 1842 by Sam Lane 1780-1859 .
Portrait exhib. RA c1842

Thomas Moor Horsford (1805-1868)

Thomas Moor Horsford (TMH) qualified as a barrister at Lincoln's Inn in 1834 and seems to have practised there. However, like many sons of hard working fathers he also seems to have fancied a more artistic life. He wrote poetry- and published. He wrote music and lyrics- and published, all of it similar to the sentimental taste of the time. In 1842 he married Phoebe Bull, whose splendid picture was exhibited at the Royal Academy. They had two children.

In about 1843, both Thomas and his wife Phoebe converted to Catholicism. His descendants remained of the Catholic Church, worshipping in Falmouth, and contributing largely to the building of the church there. It has often seemed that this particularity of faith, so strongly held, separated the later generations from others in Cornwall, suggesting a sense of isolation for his grandson Douglas and Douglas' daughter.

It seems that TMH regarded Bosvathick as his home even before his father's death, and in 1848 had a three day sale of the contents at Bosvathick, presumably so that he could modernise and upgrade the house. He also had a 'town-house' in Falmouth, which although only four miles distant was difficult by road or at night. This house at Stratton Terrace seeems to have been sold in 1860. Its contents realised £377.00, with 'many lots being withdrawn.'

IMPORTANT SALE.

CATALOGUE OF THE

VERY VALUABLE FURNITURE

AND COSTLY EFFECTS,

The Property of T. M. Horsford, Esq.

(Who is about to reside on the Continent.)

CONSISTING OF

Drawing Room Suite in the finest Wallnut;

Including,—Costly Musical Instruments; Ormolu Candelabras and Girandoles.

DINING ROOM IN THE BEST SPANISH MAHOGANY.

VALUABLE OIL PAINTINGS,

BY KNOWN MASTERS.

Superior Furniture for Library & Breakfast Parlor.

THE BED ROOM APPENDAGES

Include,—Pole and Ring and other Bedsteads; Beautiful Wardrobes; marble top Washstands, &c. And the

Usual variety of Domestic Requisites.

THE WHOLE OF WHICH WILL BE

SOLD BY AUCTION,

BY MESSRS. OLVER & SONS,

At Mr. Horsford's Town Residence,

ON STRATTON TERRACE, GREEN BANK, FALMOUTH.

Notice of the sale in 1860 of the contents of the Horsford 'townhouse'in Falmouth.

Although he had been settled at Bosvathick and had been

a magistrate for Cornwall for many years, Thomas Moor Horsford then went on a continental tour, and it is perhaps from that tour that much furniture and decoration arrived at Bosvathick. He did not long survive his return and died in 1868.

Thomas Moor Alphonse Horsford as a schoolboy. (1847-1914)

Thomas Moor Alphonse Horsford (1847-1914)

Thomas Moor Alphonse Horsford (TMAH) inherited Bosvathick in 1868 when he was only 21. He had been educated at Stoneyhurst College and joined the army in 1868, the year of his inheritance. Although he maintained a London address and Club at the Windham, he settled down in Cornwall from the 1870s. He married in 1884.

His army connections seem to have been of great importance. The library remains full of his books on training, army management and operation. He was promoted captain in 1874 and continued being promoted steadily until retiring as a Colonel in 1901. Unusually he seems to have had this rank in both the regular army and in the militia, (The Cornwall and Devon Miners Artillery) in which he remained 34 years.

A very early phtograph of the young Thomas Moor Horsford

It is clear that he was a great lover of his position in the army, which must have required much mess jollity. One or two of his humourous poems or speeches have survived. His photographs suggest he was an austere man, and we do not know how he met his wife, the daughter of a wealthy magnate from distant Glasgow. However, he and his wife were known as 'Tommy and Nellie', which suggests a friendly and sociable couple.

TMAH managed his properties and investments well. His will and estate showed that he was a very wealthy man at the time of his death, despite having spent great sums of money on the Bosvathick House and Estate. It is an extraordinary survival that the house he built remains much as he knew it, and that many of the items so meticulously listed in the inventory remain at Bosvathick today together with boxes of his correspondence, and drawers full of family photographs. His life at Bosvathick is still the basis for life today, and his enthusiasms which included automobiles and shooting are still recalled.

Ellen (Nellie) Ross Miller about the time of her marriage to TMA Horsford in 1884

TMA Horsford was said to have been of genuinely generous dispositon and 'much esteemed' by all who knew him, including his tenants.

The Sabre-tash of Colonel Thomas Moore Alphonse Horsford

Tommy and Nellie Horsford with their two sons, Gavin and Douglas.

Colonel TMA Horsford
1847-1914
An oil painting done after his death by Thomas Wood Holgate

Thomas Gavin Moor Horsford (1892-1915)

When his father died in 1914, Gavin Horsford had little time to enjoy Bosvathick. He had been educated at Beaumont School and photos show he enjoyed country life and sports. However, so soon as War was declared in 1914, he moved overseas, acting in a temporary capacity until he could formally join a regiment. Wounded and returning to England, he returned to the trenches and was killed in 1915 having been head of the family for only some nine months from 8 Sept. 1914 to his death.

His death seems to have destroyed his mother, for whom all life stopped. Books, photographs and records testify to the horrific stroke felt by the family at the death of the favorite son and heir. This must have been an emotion common to many families. The library is full of reports of the death of family friends and acquaintances, a reminder of the horror of a time when so many families lost their sons.

Colonel Thomas Moore Alphonse Horsford in old age.

Douglas Moor Horsford (1895-1983)

Douglas, who had also been to school at Beaumont had never expected to inherit. He also enjoyed the country pursuits of shooting and fishing. He may have suffered from knowing that he had never been the favorite son, and from being kept at home as long as possible rather than being able to join up. He did eventually join up, became a Captain, but saw no foreign service.

A photograph shows him leading his platoon during a victory parade in London in 1919.

It took some years to sort out the affairs of his father and mother, who herself died in 1918. After that Douglas woo'd Cora, a Horsford cousin who lived in Suffolk. She was a young war wid-

Thomas Gavin Moor Horsford, 1892-1915, photographed June 15 1915 at Givenchy the day before he was killed,

ow with two children, and he was able to offer them a new life at Bosavthick. Her two boys, Godfrey (Bunny) and Gordon Cavendish grew up at Bosvathick, where they were joined in 1924 by their half sister Corraleen Mary Moor Horsford.

Douglas presided over a changing world, and did his best to cope, adjust and maintain Bosvathick as it had been. He still has interests in Weymouth and had inherited one or two tenancies in Scotland, from his mother. He devoted much of his time to his interests, his aviary, his cars and his antique researches.

With the Second World War, he volunteered for duty, but was too old to go overseas. However he had posts in the army around Britain, but this was a lonely time and also difficult for Bosvathick House itself. The house was now bereft of staff, but had in the spare rooms of the house a number of evacuees from the bombing, ensuring a difficult and complex time of juggling for food and provisions.

His wife died in 1962, and he lived on alone for a further 21 years with the company of his daughter, and on occasion a housekeeper-companion.

Douglas was also a committed catholic, but old fashioned in his beliefs. He was not happy when the Latin Mass was abandonned and then refused to attend the church, instead paying for a special priest to come out to the house once a month to say the mass in the proper latin.

He became somewhat of a recluse as he grew older but is still remembered with affection by many.

Douglas Horsford as a young army officer

Douglas Moor Horsford
A painting by Thomas Wood Holgate

Corraleen Horsford,
One of two oil paintings by Thomas Wood Holgate, c.1942

Cora Grace Graham Horsford (Corrie) at about the time of her marriage to Douglas Horsford and then in a portait c 1942 by Thomas Wood Holgate

The combined arms of the Horsford and Moor family as from the marriage of Joseph Horsford and Phillis Moor.

Chapter 7
The Coat of Arms

One of the stained glass windows to the hall at Bosvathick carries the arms of Horsford and Moor.

The possession of a coat of arms was always a sign of status and position, and the rules closely guarded and supervised. The marriage of the Moor family to the Horsford resulted in the joining of two 'coat armour' families, and a shield which reflects the marriage of 1801 is shown on the stained glass window. Sadly, arms descend in the male line, and not to collateral branches. It is not thought that anyone at Bosvathick is still entitled to any highly decorated heraldic shield.

However heraldry is for many a fascinating and colourful record of social history. A good pun has remained an essential part of Heraldry, and most coats of arms registered over the last 800 years reflect some form of pun or reference to the family name and activities.

The Muir coat of arms was no different. It was said to originate from the story of Kenneth Moir, who accompanied Lord James Douglas to Spain around 1330 to join King Alonso XI of Spain against the 'pagan moors'. Lord Douglas died leading a charge in an attempt to rescue a colleague. Kenneth Moir fought so well in the charge, cutting off the heads of three of the enemy moors, that his friends claimed that

"One Scottish Moir can kill three pagan Moors"

This is said to be the origin of the coat of arms which shows three Moors heads with the blood dripping from their necks. The actual heraldic description is

"Three mauretanian heads, couped and distilling gutt de snag proper. Crest: A mauretanian head couped and the motto 'Major opima ferat' or Let the worthiest carry off the prize".

There were several versions for the different branches of the Muir family. This version is that of the original family, as used by James Muir of Stoneywood and his descendants.

The moor's head crest and family motto survived on much silver, plate and memorabilia, although no member of the present family is entitled to their use.

Joseph Horsford achieved his grant of arms in 1804, a compliment to his wealth and stature.

They too were much used on family articles and silver .Despite the direct line of descent, use of these arms has also died out through failure of a direct male line.

The description of the Horsford Arms is:

"Vert, on a chevron per pale argent and or, betweeen three horses heads erased of the second, three mullets pierced purpure."

The crest was *"a horse passant per pale argent and sable fording through water propre"*. The motto was *Benigno numine*, or *By the favour of the heavens*. The livery, if ever used, was *Chocolate with red plush breeches.*

This coat of arms punned the use of the Horsford name by combining horses with the water of a ford. The three mullets are thought to refer to the successful trade enjoyed by the Horsfords at sea.

The original grant of arms to the Horsford family was made in 1804. This magnificent colourful document has a fine leatherette covered box. Lost for nearly 100 years, the document was only found when breaking into a safe in which were locked the valuables of Gavin Horsford, the heir killed in 1916.

Chapter 8
The House Today

Captain Douglas and Cora Horsford

Thomas Moor Alphonse Horsford, who had rebuilt and extended the mansion at Bosvathick, died in 1914, followed shortly after by his heir, Gavin, who was killed in the trenches of the First World War. The house then passed in 1916 to the younger brother Douglas who continued to live at Bosvathick until his death in 1983.

During this long period, he enjoyed shooting, the collection of caged birds, antiques, good cars and betting on greyhounds or horses, but seems to have done little to earn a living. He was exceptionally knowledgable about antiques and dealt in them throughout his life, although without making substantial sums, and benefitng from what he could sell from the contents of the house. He tried many ways of making money, but brought up as a 'gentleman' who was not expected to work, it is not clear how he survived 67 years as owner of Bosvathick.

Corraleen Horsford,
In a photograph taken in 1950.

It is alleged that much was spent on betting and that attempts were made by his family to prevent further gambling. A note he wrote in one of his account books suggests that 'noone should enter commodity trading, unless they know something about it', presumably a reference to the triumph of hope over knowledge or ability.

In practice, his life saw the gentle decline of the estate and his fortunes. 12 farms and the remaining property around Weymouth were sold, often at values well below those of the market, since he relied on poor quality advice from 'professionals' which was not always to his benefit. The industrial estates of Falmouth, for instance were sold at a tiny proportion of their value as poor quality tenanted farms, but resold as an industrial estate within a few months.

Popular with tenants and in Cornwall, he saw himself as a paternal landlord, which meant that he did not worry too greatly about rents- but also never had the money to improve or repair his property.

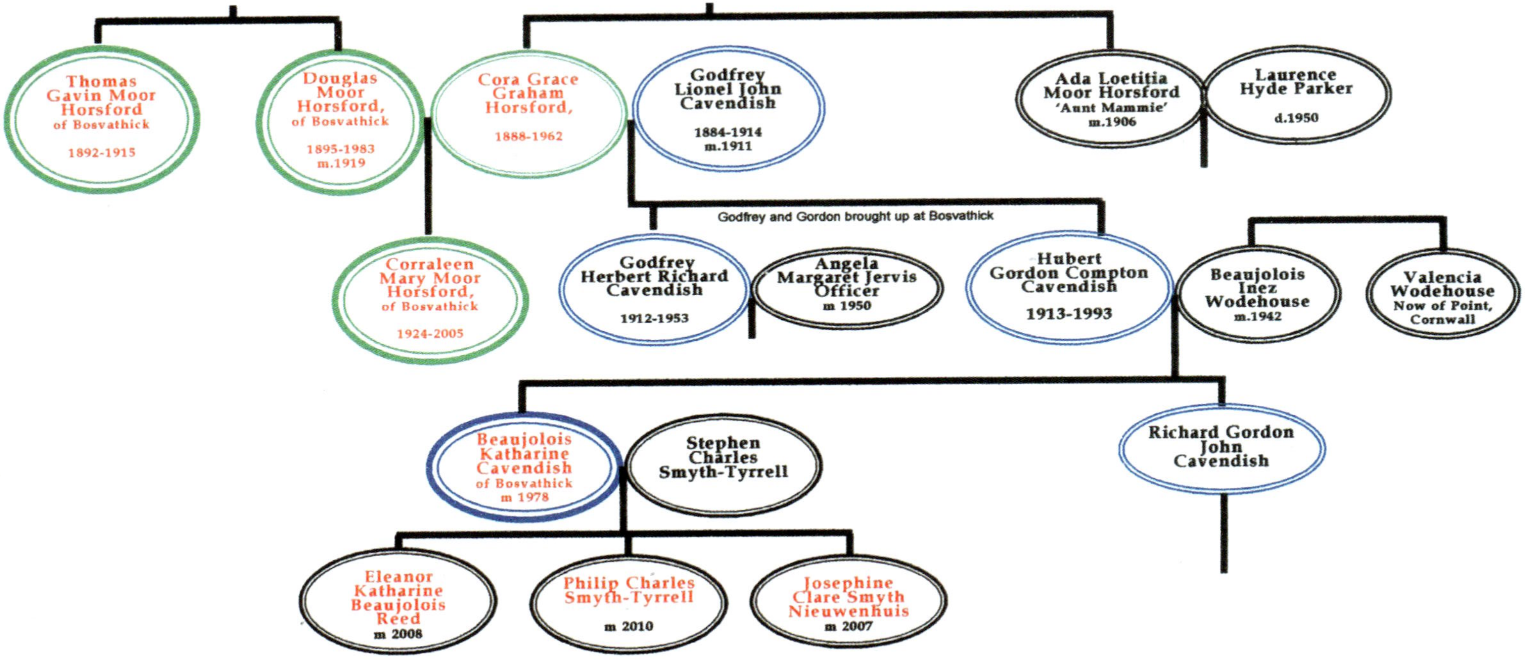

The Horsford family tree showing the change of name to Tyrrell

On his death, Bosvathick was inherited by his daughter, Corraleen Mary Moor Horsford. Corraleen had had a difficult life. Always in poor health and with long term inherited health problems, she had become the carer first for her mother and then for her ageing father. Never having gone to school, but taught by a governess, she had spent but a few nights away from Bosvathick in all her life. Save for what little she had learnt from her father, she had no experience or ability in the management of the house and tenancies and financial difficulties continued to worry her.

The Cavendish Connection.

Corraleen's Mother, Cora Horsford had lived at Bosvathick most of her life, but had arrived there with two small boys from her first marriage. The boys, brought up at Bosvathick, were themselves direct descendants of Joseph Horsford and Phillis Moor. The older boy died in 1953, but the younger, Gordon Cavendish, had lived by Bosvathick since shortly after the second world war, where he had served in Africa.

Godfrey Cavendish married Cora Horsford in 1911, served in India and died in 1914.

Gordon Cavendish had married Beaujolois Wodehouse in 1942 and brought up their two children on the estate and in Constantine. It was therefore to Gordon that Corraleen turned for advice and made the suggestion that he and Beaujolois move back into Bosvathick to provide company and to ensure that life at the house could continue. At the same time, Corraleen Horsford planned a jump in the generations so that the house would then pass to Katharine, (their daughter and her niece), and her husband Stephen Tyrrell.

Godfrey and Cora had two sons, Godfrey (Bunnie) to the left and Gordon to the right.

This move meant that some modernisation of the house became necessary. Until the mid eighties, water had been pumped from wells or tanks for both Bosvathick and the surrounding houses. Corraleen Horsford continued to drink well water to the day she died. Electricity too, had been supplied by generators in outbuildings to the dwellings of the estate. Bosvathick continued to enjoy a 'new' little Austin engine reputed to date from the first world war. This, together with a battery room full of old and inefficient cell batteries supplying a DC current was all that was available to the house. Corraleen Horsford was adept at running the old generator, and arranging for a helper to pull water from the well. A visit to the house with her at night required a complex too-ing and fro-ing to switch on a single bulb in sequence as you walked round the corridors, because of course the gen-

Gordon Cavendish married Beaujolois Wodehouse in 1942

One of the wonders of Bosvathick remains the day nursery. Every square inch of wall in this large room is papered with pictures and posters from the magazines and prints of the time. It is an astonishing record of Edwardian enthusiasms and traditions. It was done for the two boys Gavin and Douglas Horsford in about 1904

erator and batteries had limited capacity. Life without a good electricity supply or plenty of water was difficult.

Gordon and Beaujolois Cavendish and Corraleen Horsford together with Stephen and Kate Tyrrell arranged for the supply of electricity to both Bosvathick and other houses. New connections were made to the water main and in the mid-1980's, they moved in to Bosvathick House.

The house was not divided but rather shared, an arrangement that continued when, on the death of Gordon Cavendish, Stephen and Kate Tyrrell joined in living at Bosvathick House. Active in the management of the property since the mid eighties, Stephen and Kate Tyrrell brought up their three children at Bosvathick, sharing a kitchen for much of the time with Corraleen Horsford and enjoying the company of Beaujolois Cavendish also.

Katharine Cavendish on her marriage in 1978

This was a time to renovate and repair the house and its buildings after a century of neglect, and time to develop businesses which could operate from Bosvathick. It was also a time to provide improvements to a house which until the '80s had had only one bathroom. Much of that modernisation is now complete and although. like the painting of the Forth Bridge, repairs can never cease, there is now time to spend restoring and improving the gardens and grounds.

Stephen Tyrrell, about six, drawn by his mother, artist Joan Phyllis Smyth-Tyrrell

Although now lived in by an extended family, with every corner of Bosvathick well used, decoration and layout remain unaltered. This includes three reception areas and a nursery papered with prints from around 1904. Although corridors are now carpeted and there is some central heating, the house maintains that appearance it had around 1910. The house has seen few changes since then, save for the introduction of mains electricity and water. This means that not only does the layout of the rooms reflect the original purpose but that rooms such as the butler's pantry, the paraffin room continue in existence. The great glory of the house is however the decoration, furniture, clutter, paper records and ephemera. This clutter has survived from being lived in by one family for so long. Quantities of memorabilia are everywhere, and this together with an essentially Edwardian scheme of decoration ensure that the house remains an important museum of interior life and social custom.

Stephen Tyrrell painted in 2008 by Jessica Catchpole (part portrait)

However, the most notable change in the 20thC has been the complete disappearance of the staff round which the operation of the house was once designed.

Visitors to Bosvathick are greeted first, in the drawing room on the left,
and are given breakfast in the dining room shown on the right.

Bedrooms are large and comfortable, with a range of beds and layouts. Bathrooms are all modern.

Other rooms can also
be sometimes available,
including the Library.

Nowadays, a number of businesses are based at Bosvathick.
These include a bed and breakfast business run by Kate Tyrrell.

Chapter 9
Lions and Cornish Crosses

The entrance to Bosvathick showing pillars, balls and the two lions on their pedestal from a painting by Stanhope Forbes.
The entrance pillars are often painted or photographed. Another fine oil of the gates at Bosvathick is by Thomas Wood Holgate.

The entrance to Bosvathick was remade sometime around 1880. Until 1860 this had been a track from the road that went through the farmyard of Bosvarren Croft (now Little Bosvathick) to Bosvathick itself. Around 1860, Bosvarren Croft was purchased and enlarged as the Lodge to the country house of the Horsfords. Some farm buildings were removed and the drive widened and planted. This was also when the great granite boulder half way up the drive was shaped to form a seat.

In the 1880's it was thought that a new Lodge would be appropriate, and architects were asked to draw up plans. The plans- which seem sensible- were rejected in favour of a small sketch drawn by TMA Horsford on the back of an envelope, surely the only true recorded case of a house being designed on an envelope. The design was neat, if a little impractical. The new Lodge was built in the early 1880s, and given an earth closet in the garden. It has not been much altered since, and is still a charming building with central chimney stack and fish scale slates.

At around the same time, drawings were made for a grander entrance to the house. This included fine granite posts with balls and bearers, part of a collection which had built up at Bosvathick. These may have been the balls and posts that were once in the farm yard or town place of Bosvathick and formed the entrance to the garden of the 1760 house. They may have come from another of the Horsford houses or been purchased when Trewardreva in Constantine was reduced to half its size in the 1860s with much fine granite sold. It is possible these were once part of an entrance to that house.

In addition to a stile to each side, the entrance gates include two swirling decorative knees, once used on the gables of a great house, but now cut short to form decorative pieces. They may have come from Carwythenack, another great house of Constantine demolished in the 19thC through family dispute.

The two lions and their plinths may also have been found at Trewardreva. Around 1868, Polsue describes the lions as guarding the main lawn to Bosvathick. J. Roberts in his memoirs of Constantine remembered they had formed a Trewardreva entrance near Trewardreva Mill, before being moved to Bosvathick.

The southern or left hand lion at Bosvathick

The two lions are a pair, and form part of a set of which another four lions survive. Each pair in the set is a pair with one lion looking left and the other to the right.

Two of the lions are on the lawns at Trerice. These came from the Arundel family home at Lifton in Devon, where in turn they were said to have come from the earlier Arundel home at Kenegie near Penzance. Kenegie was inherited by the last Arundel of Menadarva, so long as he changed his name to Harris. There is therefore a strong tradition that the Trerice Lions are of Arundel origin. It is right that they should be in one of the greatest of Arundel houses at Trerice.

The northern or right hand lion at Bosvathick

Another two lions are now on the lawns of the National Trust house, Glendurgan near Falmouth, the home of the Fox family. They are thought to have been bought for the Fox town house at Bank House, Falmouth. One of this pair had a spell at Greatwood, before being reunited at Glendurgan. These two lions appear to have been recorded back to about 1800. They once stood each side of the entrance to Bank House.

We therefore have six lions in Cornwall, all astonishingly similar. All appear to have been made to the same dimensions (about 44” long x 22” wide and 29” high) and in the same workshop although two, slightly different, were perhaps made by a different craftsman. They have similar claws and paws, six ribs each and a tassell to their tails. They seem to have been carved by men not that familiar with either a real lion or their picture. The granite is fine grained and unlike much found around Kenegie. The granite was not quarried so must be of some age, and the carvings are much damaged by wind erosion. It has been suggested that the erosion represents some 500 years of wear.

Finally, I believe that each lion has a barrel chest, or is holding a shield, both of which would be suitable for heraldic decoration.

Many dates have been proposed for them. Are they prehistoric, ancient Egytian, medieval 17thC or 18thC in origin? The origin of these six lions will remain a mystery.

It seems likely that the six had been at Kenegie until William Arundell (later Harris) moved to Lifton around 1820. Perhaps he moved only one pair all that way and the other four (shown in an undated drawing by Thomas Allom of the Kenegie summer house) were sold, two going to the Foxes at Bank House and two going to the Trewren family at Trewarvdreva. This house was partially demolished and the contents and ornaments sold by their descendants around 1860.

A celtic cross mounted on a rockery. One of three at Bosvathick

G.M.Trinick thought that the Lions might have been designed for use at Kenegie, but was unable to identify sufficient plinths for all six. It would be nice to imagine that all six were genuine Arundel Lions and had originated not at Kenegie, but at that other great Arundel house, Menadarva, of which now only part remains. They may also have decorated the much earlier great house at Kenegie which is known to have had three entrances, each suitable for a pair of lions.

The original site and date may never be identified, but the most likely theory is that they formed part of an avenue or steps of heraldic lions and that they were carved as part of the 14thC enthusiasm for heraldic emblems and display.

No matter what their history, they are a unique and delightful entrance to Bosvathick.

Further up the drive are three Celtic Crosses placed on and by a rockery and pond by TMA Horsford in the late 19thC. These 'ancient monuments' are rare items and particularly rare as a garden group. There is some uncertainty as to where they had been found. Old maps show one as near the mainhouse. Another could have been marking the way across the stream beween Bosvathick and Trevaney. There was a possible cross at Roscollas. Family records say one or two were found at Trewoon, or that one or two may have come from Bosvarren.

The crosses are fairly crudely carved. Their function is still debated but it seems accepted that they are of 8th or 9thC date and were used as either or both of boundary or way markers on tracks to the church. They were probably essential to the 9thC system of area administration. It may be relevant that Bosvathick is right on the edge of the parish and its boundary markers.

The crosses have been carefully recorded. Their continuing health is occasionally checked by officials; to us, they are an essential part of the garden.

Like many other Cornish gardens, Bosvathick has many magnolias, rhododendron, azaleas and other plant specimens scattered around the grounds or planted in decorative clumps separated by trees or laurel.

Between March and the end of May, Bosvathick has weeks of snowdrops followed by swathes of primroses and prairies of bluebells

Part of the Haha which bordered the park or Warren between the house and the lake.

The grounds also have much carved granite stonework rescued from the earlier Elizabethan house on the site. To the left is a garden arch, once the front door of the farmhouse; a second now forms the entrance to the kitchen yard (centre). On the right is a flight of steps, some of which once led to the first front door but now lead to a considerable collection or avenue of carved granite.

Chapter 10
Gardens and Outbuildings

Bosvathick started life as a small farm hamlet on a plateau protected by a ridge from bad weather to the south west. Here were two farms each with buildings, and a central yard or 'townplace' between them.

The bigger of the two houses was adapted to become Bosvathick House, and the other farm continued as the home farm until 1880.

Although there was work to the gardens and drives, we have few records of any changes before TMA Horsford took over in 1868. Outside, the gardens are mainly informal lawn and shrub.

He seems first to have added a conservatory to the southwest, and then developed a small stable block to the west. In rebuilding this little coach house, used as an apple store and work shop for most of its life, he used as a partition the original Georgian timber front door of the house, not used when the old front door was changed. This door has now been repaired and used in the stable offices for the house.

The old front door to Bosvathick now in use in the estate office. Dating from the 1760s it is large wide and heavy and with three massive remade hinges, holes for a large knocker and for a timber lock box and massive key. In its original position it had a top light above it.

Around 1868 it is thought that the lions, now at the gate, were first placed at the entrance to the lawn. In 1865 a plan shows an extended garden and proposals for the improvement of the drive.

In 1857 the little farm to the east of the entrance, now called Little Bosvathick, had been purchased, and during the 1860s received a new wing and other alterations and a new entrance to the public road. Works also included the removal of the farm buildings that had been both sides of the drive and the building of walls and planting of trees to cut the little farm off from the Bosvathick entrance.

This had been intended to be the Lodge to the house, but was too far from the road. Proposals were sought for a new lodge to the west of the entrance. The first Architect's plans for Bosvathick Lodge were aban-

Plans for a new stable block were prepared and tenders invited in 1887. The date works were completed is not certain. The drawing to bottom right was one supplied with a tender for fittings.

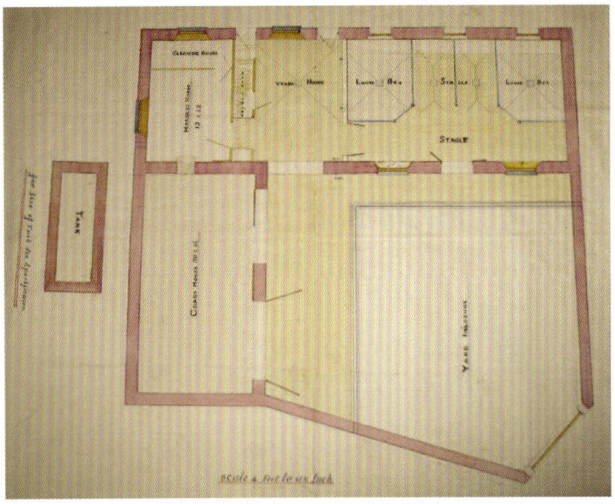

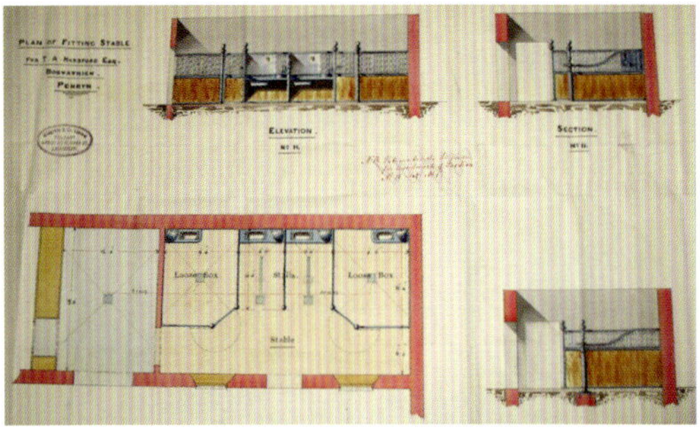

Around 1880, TMA Horsford decided to demolish the farmhouse and buildings to the southwest of the Bosvathick house and lay out a new model farm and farmhouse a couple of fields to the south. The magnificent house and farm buildings still stand.

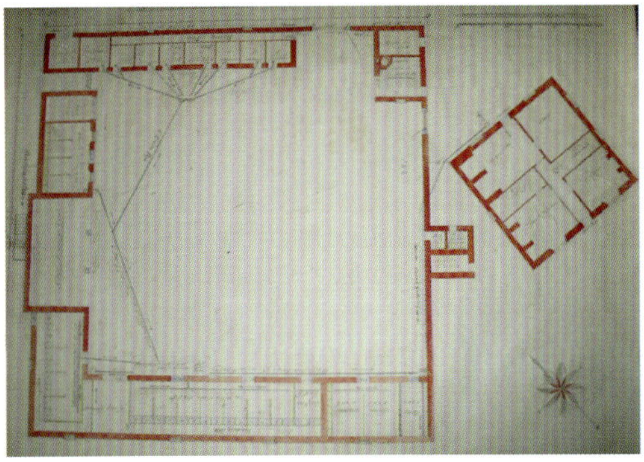

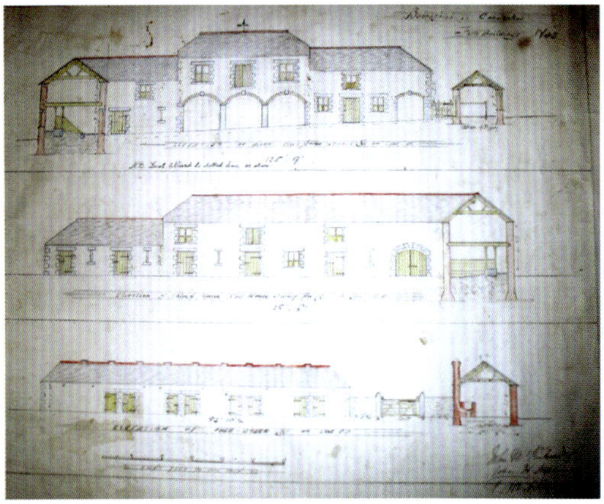

This is a sketch done by TMA Horsford on the back of an envelope dated 1884.

The Lodge in 1990 remains identical to the original plans and save for modern facilities and a larger garden, is still so today.

doned, perhaps because of cost and looks. So therefore, unlike other building works carried out at Bosvathick, no plans for the Lodge exist. It seems that the new design really did originate with the sketch done on the back of an envelope by TMA Horsford in 1884. John Rowe, a local builder then went on to draw up plans and elevations, based on this sketch. The estimates from John Trethowan, mason and John Rowe carpenter came to £162.00 The eventual bill for the building of the Lodge between September 1884 and May 1885 came to some £210.00.

In 1880, it was decided to provide gardens appropriate to a 'countryseat', and to remove the home farm, reorganise the garden and change the route of the drives. This work resulted in the defining of the present garden by stone hedges, the alteration of the drive to its present position, the removal of the little wall, pillars and forecourt before the house, the terracing of the site of the old farm to the northwest as garden and provision of a great lawn and other garden features like a rockery and sunken garden. One well was covered in and the new south lawn levelled and remade. Along the drive, cast iron railings were erected, with a long Haha to allow the visitor uninterrupted views of the countryside.

Outside the grounds, new tracks and plantations were established partly to cover the quarries from which stone had been obtained for the houses, but also to provide a landscape appropriate for the house.

For the next century, the family worried about the wind and privacy, so they developed banks of laurel and orcuba to shelter their shrubs and plants. Never plantsmen as were other Cornish landowners, the Horsfords nevertheless enjoyed gardening and placed it high in their interest. The last two women Horsfords, Cora and her daughter Corraleen were keen and indeed exceptionally knowledgable about plants. It was unfortunate that fear of the wind and of pruning ensured that through their lifetime, the garden became completely overgrown.

In the 1890s was completed a substantial stable and coach block, designed to incorporate the best materials and ideas of the time. However the almost immediate purchase of a motor car ensured that the coachhouse too is uniquely untouched and in its original design condition.

Behind this large building were granite pigsties for the house pig, and great wood sheds for fuel. Beyond this again was set up a new kitchen garden, although this must always have been a poor site, since it is on the top of the hill to the north. Before long a new kitchen garden was cut out of the land to the west, with to the south of that again, an extension to the garden with space for a tennis court. The tennis court remained available- but unused for nearly 80 years and it is only in 2011 that re-planting and use as part of the garden has started.

Once the main house was rebuilt from 1896 onwards, few changes were made to the grounds or outbuildings.

Douglas Horsford added a lake in the 1920s by excavating the valley bottom to the north east of the house and building a massive earth dam across the valley. This small valley is suitable as a lake since the underlying ground is a mass of waterproof St Austell clay. The lake had two islands, but soon silted up, and it is only in the last few years that it has once more been twice dredged and cleaned and is now looking fine. An entrance dock allows boats to be launched to view the islands and admire the geese, ducks and moorhens which now make this lake their home.

Douglas Horsford also added or converted buildings as Aviaries, and his daughter always had a small greenhouse, to which his step-son Gordon Cavendish added a large greenhouse.

The grounds of Bosvathick had become overgrown and it has only been in the last five years that clearance, exploration and repair has been possible. Repair has also continued on the houses and outbuildings of the estate, none of which had had material repair in the previous 100 years. Since the mid-eighties, work of modernisation, reroofing and improvement has continued non-stop It is now possible to admire many fine old buildings, with some conversions and new uses.

Bosvathick is fortunate to enjoy a traditional and little altered setting which looks set fair for the future.

Melllinzeath is a small thatched miller's house deep in the woods which was completely rebuilt in the early 1990s. It retains all the features of the 1666 rebuild and is a popular and unusual additon to estate interests.

Chapter 11
Carriages and Cars

Wheeled traffic was rare in Cornwall until the 18thC, with most goods being taken by pack horse along narrow trails. The Trewinnard Coach, famously used by the Harris Family as a social symbol to make the one mile journey to church each Sunday in the mid 18thC was famous because use of such a coach was rare. New roads for mining or quarry products and the building of Toll roads meant that families could use other carriages than small farm carts for getting about.

Geach, a smartly dressed coachman holds Jonathan the horse as TMA Horsford prepares to leave Bosvathick.

We do not know what early vehicles were used at Bosvathick. However around 1880 a new stable was made out of the farm buildings of Bosvathick Farm when that was rebuilt elsewhere. This stable had one roomy carriage house, two loose boxes, two stables and a tack room. It was not used for long, before it was replaced by a new and splendid great stable block, designed in the late 1880s. Today, the older stable has been converted to a comfortable estate office for five people. The building retains all the old stable features inside, although the central roof lantern must one day be reinstated.

Geach prepares to drive away with Mrs Horsford, who is seen in the porch with Thomas, the butler. The horses are Jonathan and Brownie. The foot scraper in the RH corner is still in use in 2011.

The new stable block was designed for carriages, horses, tack rooms, wash house, hay loft, carpenters shop and chauffeur's flat. Sadly, it was completed only four or five years before the arrival of the motor car, which did not need all these facilities. The new stable block therefore was used as a store, with all the new stable fittings, loose boxes and fine tack room remaining as new. The building remains almost unused and as designed. It did have a period as an aviary in the 1920s but also acquired a range of early motoring tools. On one door is a record of service and work to the early cars, itself a reminder of how difficult those early vehicles might be.

The ownership of a carrriage was always a matter of pride and social competition. Just as we may enjoy a powerful sports car, so the carriage was both a status symbol and a source of satisfaction and pride. The first two pictures here show two early carriages, photographed around 1890, shortly before the purchase of the first car.

The early cars were of course driven by a chauffeur and his uniform coat with Horsford buttons still exist- although rather moth eaten. Neither Colonel or Mrs Horsford drove themselves before the first world war.

The three early cars registered to Bosvathick are recorded as:

1. AF 358: A Rover 6 hp 2 seater in dark green registered 13.07.1908 to Colonel TMA Horsford.
2. AF 675: A Maudslay 17hp 26 cwt in green and black with a landulet -cabriolet body.This car was registered to Mrs Horsford on 17.05.1911.
3. AF 1171: Alldays and Onions 12hp 2 seater in green registered 27.11.1913 to Mrs Horsford.

The photographs show that the vehicles were a source of pride, although difficult to drive and with roads not suitable for cars. We have a letter from TMA Horsford complaining about the main road past Lamanva, about a mile from Bosvathick. Here in June, he wrote, there were still some 47 deep pools of water in a hundred yard stretch, destroying the springs of car and carriage.

On the almost empty roads of the time, a two car smash must have been unusual, which is why, perhaps we have much detail on an accident. Mrs TMA Horsford was being driven by Fred Stevens, the Chauffeur, when a 'big car' driven by Major Wallace came out of the Roskrow turning without looking. By sheer chance a passing phottook this photograph of the crash on the almost empty roads. A second picture clearly showed that the Major was on the wrong side of the road. This evidence was enough to clear the Chauffeur and stop an early example of road rage from Major Wallace.

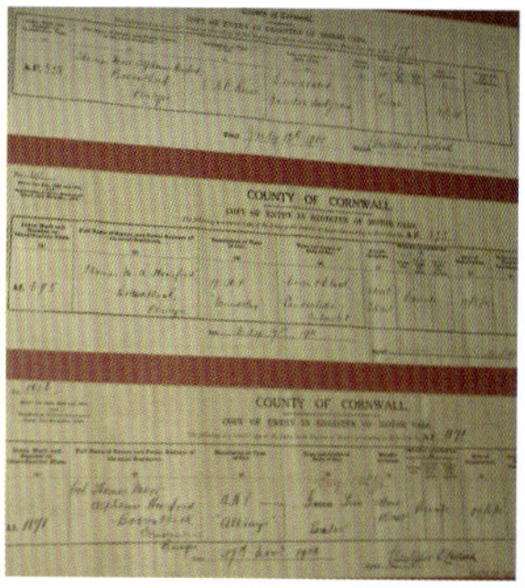

The original registration certificates for the pre-1914 automobiles.

The Rover 6 horse power 2 seater in dark green.

Stevens, the Chauffeur, with the Maudeslay in 1910. The Maudslay Motor Company was a subsidiary of AEC of Southall.It was said that the Maudslay was a pig to start, and that the ignition had to be well advanced because the car had a 'kick like a mule'.

Chapter 12
House and Staff Life

Bosvathick House was designed to provide comfort with staff to look after the needs of the family. To this end, the design reflects the social attitudes of the late 19thC, with a clear division of house and grounds between those areas for family use and those for staff.

This was never a house with great numbers of staff. although before the First World War it was laid out for a Governess, Butler, Cook/housekeeper, a parlour maid and kitchen maid. All these would expect to live in, and in addition extra help would be sought locally for help who walked in each day. In addition there were gardeners and a coachman or chauffeur, which last lived on site. This is quite a number of staff- but not considerable when compared with other houses. Douglas, who grew up before 1914 and lived to 1983, must have found it difficult to adapt to a different style of life. Indeed we know that it was necessary for the family to learn to cook, and of the sorrow the absence of a butler meant. That absence may have been a blessing in disguise, since the last butler, who left around 1939 was said to drink. Certainly there are 39 decanter stoppers, without bottles, whose breakage is attributed to him.

One of three glass cases of oddments, meant to encourage conversation and a reminder of terrible 'Sunday visiting'.

A row of poular novels, the Mills and Boon of their time.

At Bosvathick we have some idea how the family spent their time, because so much of the clutter of those lives is still available. The men had their field sports, the women had visiting. Both had a library, much of which is a snap shot of tastes around 1910. There are books on law, self help, peerages, and natural history. There are also lots of 'popular' novels, now impossible to read and so really quite collectible. Upstairs a fireplace (later removed) had playing card tiles. This and the boxes of games and cards reflect the hours spent playing cards. The unusual playing card tiles have been preserved and are still at Bosvathick.

The tiled fireplace in a guest bedroom.

Music was a big interest. Harp music from the

1840s is still in the house together with hundreds of song sheets, some written by TM Horsford and others part of Cora's much used collection. Family water colours have also survived, although none are of any quality.

Before the 1840s, the family could consider a direct association with the life of the farm. There are comments like 'The cow won't milk' in letters. This 'taking part' then vanished. As late as 1950, when Douglas Horsford tried his hand at running one of the small farms, he still had a 'hind' or manager, to do the work.

Much of the value of Bosvathick lies in its archive which includes a mass of paper reflecting the activities of nearly 200 years. There are school books and text books running from the mid 18thC onwards, thousands of photographs, small items like the silhouettes which reflect changing fashion, business papers, and the contents of several desks, advertisments, ephemera and much that

Examples of sentimental songs and lyrics composed by Thomas Moor Horsford.

A silhouette of Col TMA Horsford, aged about 3, or before he had moved into trousers.

A group in gas marks were intended to show the lighter side of army and militia training.

Country sports were a big element of life: Gavin Horsford is to the left and Douglas, with the creel, to the right.

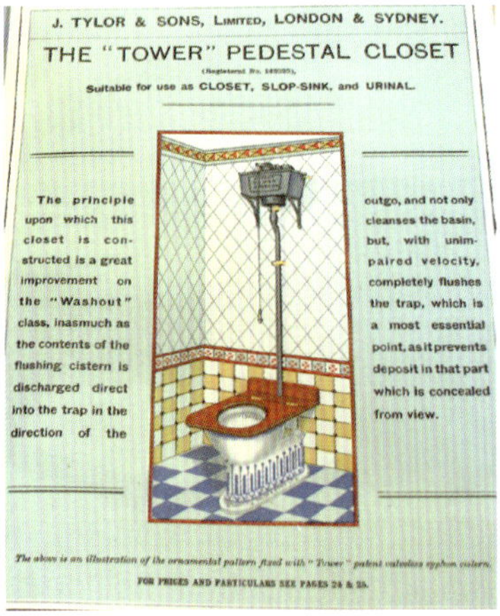

J. TYLOR & SONS, LIMITED, LONDON & SYDNEY.

THE "TOWER" PEDESTAL CLOSET

Suitable for use as CLOSET, SLOP-SINK, and URINAL.

The principle upon which this closet is constructed is a great improvement on the "Washout" class, inasmuch as the contents of the flushing cistern is discharged direct into the trap in the direction of the outgo, and not only cleanses the basin, but, with unimpaired velocity, completely flushes the trap, which is a most essential point, as it prevents deposit in that part which is concealed from view.

FOR PRICES AND PARTICULARS SEE PAGES 24 & 25.

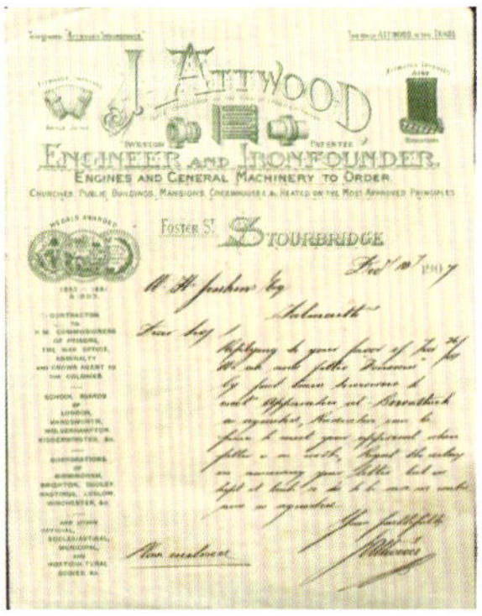

J. ATTWOOD

ENGINEER AND IRONFOUNDER

ENGINES AND GENERAL MACHINERY TO ORDER

FOSTER ST. STOURBRIDGE

Bundles of documents, trade correspondence and the catalogues from which the rebuilt house was furnished in 1896 are some of the thousands of documents which have yet to be sorted.

gives us a direct link to the life of the 19thC.

Bosvathick was a house divided by 'green doors' which separated those areas used by the family from those of the staff and of service rooms. In common with most other houses of the time, children were the 'other' side of the green doors. Bosvathick had both a large day nursery and night nursery in a wing as far as possible from the rooms of the owners.

This layout meant lots of dark cold concrete corridor. Every room had a fireplace, of which many were made up each day, cleaned and kept supplied with coal from the three bunkers designed for different grades of coal, the ash being taken to a purpose built ash pit.

It was also a house without bathrooms, but with a wash room for the distribution of jugs and bowls in the morning and the removal of pots and potties. This last was the duty of a junior maid. Still living in Constantine is a lady whose first job was, at the age of 14, to walk the two miles from her home to Bosvathick, there to creep along the servants' path out of sight of the windows round to the back door and once there, help out the housemaid. Her work included the emptying of chamberpots, the bringing of water to the wash stands in the bedrooms and the carrying of coals to the rooms.

Below is a copy of a card, prepared for a 'Tweenie' or junior maid and listing her hours and duties. It looks like hard work.

Douglas and Cora Horsford with Godfrey and Gordon Cavendish show that visits were mde to the sea, even if they were a trifle formal.

For much of the 20thC, life at Bosvathick reflected difficulties of finance and social change, but there were still parties and amusements.

Between Maid's Work

Note: This maid was known as 'The Tweenie'

8.00 - Kitchen breakfast.
8.30-9.00- Porch.
9.00-9.30- Servants bedrooms.
9.30-10.00- Help cook wash up.
10.00 - Go to bedrooms, grates and help housemaid bedside.
11.30 - Lunch.
12.00 - Help cook with vegetables.
Sweep back landing and stairs or scrub back porch and passage or kitchen according to days work.
2.00 - Kitchen dinner.
2.30 - Wash up dinner things and finish passage or other work.
4.15 - Change into black dress and lay kitchen tea at 5.00.
5.45 - Do vegetables for dinner.
Then go to linen room for work till 2nd gong rings.
9.00 Supper.
10.00 Bed.
General: Carry dishes during dinner to butlers table.
Wash up dinner things with cook, lay table.
The time between 12.30 and 2.00 can be used either for cleaning back stairs etc or turning out a room, or cleaning cans or washing or any other work.

Much of this life is now strange to us. For instance Bosvathick was designed with strong bars to all windows on the ground floor. Although this may have been to protect against burglary it must have given a gloomy impression to staff and to visitors.

The cook was issued with the foods and stores, rice, spices and basic food stuffs from the chatelaine's store room, a room filled with shelves and drawers of interest. Each day the issue was made through a little low window to the corridor. The window is still there.

With no modern implements, laundry washing, wringing and pressing all took hours. However, a staff earth closet was supplied for use by staff, and it was only some 100 yds from the kitchen door.

Security grilles give a gloomy look to the windows.

The little window through which supplies were given out each day by the lady of the house.

There are no longer any staff at Bosvathick. However, in 2005 a full complement of approriately dressed volunteers supporting a charity event for the cathedral helped give us some idea of what life was like.

A recently restored single seat earth (not water) closet for staff use.

Lamps in the paraffin room, two of many which were either plain or decorative and waiting to be relit.

The wired bell system reused in the rebuilding of 1896 stretch around the house to allow staff to be called. Many of the bells still work, and one or two have recently been refurbished.

Chapter 12
Cooking and a Recipe from Bosvathick

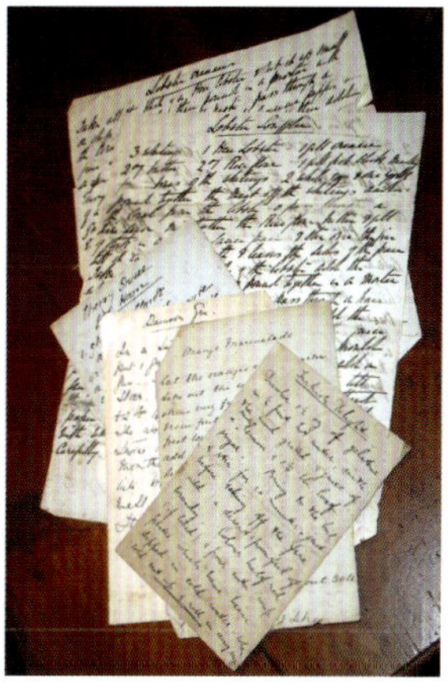

A selection of old recipes from Bosvathick

Until the end of the 18thC few recipes were written down. Methods of cooking were considered either common knowledge, or the 'secret' trade and skill of the cook. Recipes were of no interest to the literate gentry and those who could read and write tended not to work in the trade of cook. We therefore have few records of what was eaten in the ordinary as opposed to grand households. Such recipes as survive are usually for meals of magnificence or the unusual.

Some gentry houses have kept books or bundles of recipes, although not so many have survived as might be expected, because cooking recipes were considered the private information and secret of the cook. Those that survive were often those kept by the Lady of the House, who did not of course cook for herself, but who wished to be able to offer specialities to guests or record some particular family favourite.

Since cooking was regarded as a specialist activity, it was the management of the cook that was seen as of importance. One has only to read the memoirs and records of the gentry through the last two centuries to realise how much of a mystery the work of the kitchen remained until after the Second World War. That war spelt the end of 'service' and of cooks. Where before the war, those employed 'in service' were a significant part of the working population, this had become almost insignificant by the time Queen Elizabeth came to the throne.

The recipes therefore tend to be the special or the extraordinary. Late Victorian recipes might include exotic starters ('*take 12 cock lobsters*'), soups for the invalid, recipes for many different scented waters, or for antimacasar mixtures, as well as for sweet puddings and sweet side dishes. Basic cooking for main courses was not listed unless you included the infinite ways for curing ham, or of dealing with offal.

Bosvathick had always had a cook, and in the days after the second world war the family felt helpless without one. There are bundles of recipes meant to eke out rationing, and bundles of recipes where the family where clearly learning to cook. The Bosvathick recipes that survive are all in a range of writings but kept by the Mistress as her private record and for special occasions. The control of and cooking on the range was always considered an art and the arrival of the simpler AGA considered a great boon. Cooking and recipes were also affected by different methods for supply and storing of food.

The recipes included soufflés, creams, substantial puddings, exotic fish dishes, syllabubs, vegetable marrow jam, a cherry sauce for ham, mincemeat or an anchovy savoury.

One of the difficulties with choosing recipes is that tastes have changed. The recipes that survive from the 19thC all tend to be too rich and too sweet for our taste. We have chosen three examples from the papers at Bosvathick.

Orange Marmalade

This remains the family recipe of choice and one that has been much enjoyed. However, I am told it has some unusual components and proportions. Publication of details was forbidden.

Turkish Delight

Dissolve 1½ oz of gelatine in ½ pint hot water, [together] with the rind grated, the juice of a small lemon and 1¼ lbs loaf sugar.

Bring to the boil and stir for 20 minutes.

Just before taking off the fire add a dessertspoonful of brandy.

Colour half red (if liked) and pour into soup plates which have been dipped in cold water.

When cold cut up and roll in icing sugar.

Damson Gin- one of many alchoholic concoctions.

In a two gallon jar put 1 gallon of unsweetened gin – 3 quarts of damsons or sloes, ½ oz bitter almonds and 2lbs loaf sugar.

The above to be shaken twice a week for two months, then strain into bottles and cork well and the longer kept the better.

MENU

Clear Soup

Chicken Fricassee

Roast Mutton

Orange Cream.
Chantilly Baskets

Aspic Eggs.

A sample menu for dinner in the dining room, attended by the butler.

Lobster Soufflé

The recipe we chose to cook was for a Lobster Soufflé, which has been copied out as originally written.

We tried this using a 2kg lobster, but found that such a lobster went a long way. Unable to find a hen lobster, we used a cock lobster and substituted lump fish roe for the coral of a hen lobster.

Pounding the lobster into small pieces appears to be important, and it could be worth considering use of a power mixer.

The black grains in the soufflé picture are the lumpfish roe, which would not normally show, were a lobster's coral to be used.

You may need to use modern, easier methods than steaming for raising the soufflé. You could consider using grease proof paper round the soufflé dish, standing tall, in order to encourage the rising of the soufflee. The soufflé was cooked for an hour at 190°C.

The dish was delicious, but quite rich. It is better used as an appetizer, rather than a main course.

A small cock lobster ready to be cooked. The whiting have been filleted. A pot of lumpfish roe replaces the hen-lobster's 'coral' or roe.
The fish stock was made from a piece of whiting and existing fish stock.

Warning: this is quite a rich and filling dish.

The recipe follows on the next page.

A Lobster Soufflé, ready to be served.

Lobster Soufflé

A recipe from Mrs Horsford's recipe sheets,
as written out around 1870

Requirements

3 Whitings
1 Hen Lobster
1 gill Cream
2oz Butter
2 oz rice flour
1 gill fish stock made from bones of the Whitings
2 whole eggs and one yolk

Preparation

1. Pound together the meat of the Whitings with the coral from the Lobster and pass through a fine sieve.
2. Mix together the Rice Flour, butter and a gill of stock in a small saucepan. Stir over the fire till it is thick and smooth and leaves the side of the pan.
3. Take the meat of the body of the lobster add the whiting and the panada. (*Panada* is understood as a word that refers to the roux mixture made in items 1 & 2).
4. Pound together in a mortar adding the eggs one at a time. Pass through a fine sieve (this process may be omitted).
5. Add the cream whipped, a little Cayenne pepper and the juice of half a lemon.
6. Well butter a plain soufflee mould. Put a layer of the mixture in the bottom then add a few pieces of meat from the claws, repeat this until the mould is fully filled.
7. Cover with buttered paper and steam fully for half an hour.

Serving

Serve hot with white sauce poured over.
(Turn out of the tin carefully and serve quickly).

Sources and references

Principal sources and references.

The Bosvathick Archive, Bosvathick
Richard Carew of Antonie, esq: The Survey of Cornwall 1602
County Record Office: Trelowarren papers
Dunkin, Edwin Hadlow Wise: The Monumental Brasses of Cornwall 1882
Gilbert, C.S. An Historical Survey of Cornwall, Ackerman, London. 2 vols. 1817 & 1820
Gilbert, D, 1838. The Parochial History of Cornwall (4 volumes) Nicholls, London.
Includes historical notes by Hals and Tonkin
Henderson, Charles Royal Institution of Cornwall: Henderson Papers
Henderson, C., 1935. A History of the Parish of Constantine in Cornwall
Edited by Revd G H Doble For RIC 1937
Lake's Parochial History of Cornwall written by Joseph Polsue c 1865-1872 4 volumes
This includes: William Hals (1655-1737) Parochial Histories unpublished 1737
Thomas Tonkin, (1680-1742) unpublished 1742,
Langdon, Andrew Stone Crosses in West Cornwall Federation of Old Cornwall Societies 1999
D & S Lyson's Parochial History (1814) Cornwall (Volume 111 for Cornwall)
Moir, Alexander L The Moir Genealogy: A compendium of early books and references
to the Moir families: Shelf-Life Reprint
Moule, Thomas The English Counties Delineated: or, A Topographical Description of England, 1838
Padel, O.J. Cornish Place-Name Elements, English Place-Name Society, Vol 56/57, Nottingham 1985
Penaluna, Helston.1824 The History of Cornwall (2 volumes)
Stoate, TL, Hearth Tax Returns for Cornwall
Trinick, G.M. The Arundel Lions RICS 1972, updated SCSTyrrell 1995
Trefusis papers: Private collection
SCSTyrrell Personal papers, records and photographs.